When God Carries a Woman Through the Fire

Finding God's Strength in Seasons of Pain, Battle, and Becoming

Dr. Lende Click

Dedication

This book is dedicated first to my Lord and Savior, **Jesus Christ**,
the One who carried me through every fire,
held me through every sorrow,
and never left me alone.

To the **Father**, who loved me and drew me near,
to **Jesus**, who saved me and walks with me,
and to the **Holy Spirit**, who comforts, teaches, and strengthens me
day by day.

I also dedicate this book to every woman
who has cried in silence,
walked through rejection,
carried pain no one else could see,
and still chose to keep trusting God.

May you know that you are seen,
you are loved,
and you were never alone in the fire.

And to the precious children in **Cebu, Philippines**,
you are close to my heart.
May God's love surround you,
His hand guide you,
and His goodness shine upon your lives.

"When thou walkest
through the fire,
thou shalt not be burned;
neither shall the flame
kindle upon thee."

Isaiah 43:2

Author's Note

Dear Reader,

This book was written from a place of prayer, pain, healing, and deep gratitude to God.

There are some fires in life that change a woman forever. Some are seen by others, and some are carried quietly in the deepest places of the heart. There are fires of rejection, sorrow, betrayal, weakness, loneliness, and loss. There are also the hidden fires that only God fully understands.

I know something about those fires.

As I look back over my life, I can see the faithfulness of God in every season. He did not always keep me from the fire, but He never left me in it alone. He carried me, strengthened me, refined me, healed me, and taught me to trust Him more deeply. This book is my testimony of that truth.

My prayer is that these pages will comfort the hurting woman, strengthen the weary woman, encourage the rejected woman, and remind every reader that God is still near. I pray that through these chapters, you will see not only the pain of the fire, but also the love, mercy, and sustaining grace of the God who walks with us through it.

This book is also written with a sincere desire to point hearts to **Jesus Christ**. He is still Savior. He is still Healer. He is still

Deliverer. He is still the One who restores broken places and gives beauty for ashes.

Wherever you are in your journey right now, I want you to know this:
God sees you.
God hears you.
God loves you.
And if you belong to Him, you are never alone in the fire.

With love and prayer,
Dr. Lende Click

Table of Contents

Introduction
When the Fire First Came

My fire began on **June 12, 1981**, the day I accepted Jesus Christ as my Lord and Savior. Even now, forty-five years later, I still remember that sacred moment as if it had just happened. I can still feel it. It was as though a holy heat came over me from the top of my head down to the soles of my feet. It was fire, yet it did not burn. It was the presence of God. In that moment, I knew my life would never be the same again.

Before that day, I was raised in the Catholic faith, and as a little girl, I thought God was only inside the church. My mother would often remind me, "God can see you," and she taught me to fear the Lord from the time I was very young. I prayed to Him even then. I called on my Jesus the best way I knew how. But no one had ever clearly told me that Jesus died for me, that He is the Mediator between God and people, and that I could receive Him personally as my Lord and Savior.

Then came the day when everything changed.

With all the sincerity of my heart, I told God that I wanted to accept Jesus Christ as my Lord and Savior. In that holy moment, something eternal happened inside me. What I had known in part, I now knew in truth. What I had once approached from a distance, I now received personally. Jesus was no longer someone I knew about. He became the Savior I knew, the Lord I loved, and the One who would forever change my life.

When I came home, I no longer wanted to live by routine or empty tradition. I did not want religion without relationship. I wanted **Him**. I wanted to talk to Him, seek Him, adore Him, and tell Him how much I loved Him. As I grew in faith, I came to understand that God is not confined to a church building. He is everywhere. And when we receive Jesus Christ, He comes to dwell within us. He lives in me, and I am a temple of the living God.

At that time, I did not even own a Bible. The only person I knew who had one was the priest. So, I asked my mother to buy me a Bible, and we went to a Protestant store. I had never been in a place like that before. But from that day on, God placed within me a deep hunger for His Word, and that hunger has never left me. I still long for Him. I still seek Him. I still love to worship Him. There is still a fire in my soul for the presence of the Lord.

Life has not been without trials. I have walked through suffering, sorrow, and seasons of fire. But with all my heart, I believe what Scripture shows us through Shadrach, Meshach, and Abednego that God does not always keep us out of the fire, but He is faithful to be with us in it. There is a Fourth Man in the fire, and He is the Fourth Man in my fire too. I am never alone. Jesus is with me. Whatever I have faced, and whatever I may yet face, He is in me, and He has never left me.

I thank the Father for drawing me to His Son. I thank my Lord and Savior Jesus Christ for dying for me, saving me, and loving me with an everlasting love. I thank the Holy Spirit for living inside me and guiding me day by day. I believe in the Father, the Son, and the Holy Spirit, and I love Him with all my heart. I sing to Him not only on Sunday, but every day. There is not a day that I do not talk to Him, think about Him, seek Him, or worship Him. He is the breath of my life, the joy of my soul, and the One my heart longs for above all else.

I love telling others the good news. Even when people do not want to hear it, I still want them to know that Jesus loves them. I want them to know that He saves, He heals, He restores, and He is coming again. My desire is to keep growing in faith, to keep the fire burning, and to become more and more like Jesus. I want people to see Jesus in me. That is my prayer. That is my deepest desire.

I believe the Holy Spirit is our greatest Teacher. People can make mistakes, but God never does. That is why I have always wanted children and others to know the truth of God's Word for themselves. I know what it is to be hungry. I know what it is to go without. I know what it feels like to need more than this world can offer. And because of that, God has placed a burden in my heart for children, especially in the Philippines, to have food, to learn, and to know the love of God. I do not want them to know only about survival. I want them to know the Savior.

I do not want to talk about what I have done. I want to talk about what God has done in my life. His grace has carried me. His mercy has sustained me. His fire has kept me. And even now, I still pray that I will remain rooted and grounded in His love, filled with holy passion, burning with zeal, and always ready to tell the world how good God is.

I would rather be considered strange by this world than to grow cold toward Christ. I want to stay on fire for the Lord. I want to follow Him fully, love Him deeply, obey Him faithfully, and live in a way that points others to Jesus. Until the day He returns, I want my life to keep declaring this beautiful truth: **Jesus saves, Jesus loves, and Jesus is coming again.**

This is the fire that began in me on June 12, 1981. And by the grace of God, it is still burning.

Chapter 1

The Woman Who Feels Rejected

Rejection is one of the deepest fires a woman can walk through.

It wounds quietly. It does not always leave visible scars, but it leaves pain in places only God can reach. Rejection can make a woman question her worth, her beauty, her purpose, and even her place in the world. It can come from family, friends, marriage, ministry, childhood, or people we once trusted. Sometimes it comes through cruel words. Sometimes it comes through silence. Sometimes it comes through being overlooked, left out, abandoned, or made to feel as though we are not enough.

A woman who has been rejected often learns how to smile while carrying pain no one else can see. She may continue moving, serving, giving, and loving, all while silently wondering, *Why was I not wanted? Why was I not chosen? Why was I not loved the way I needed to be loved?*

But rejection does not have the final word. God does.

One of the women in Scripture who understood rejection was **Hagar**.

Hagar's story is painful. She was used, mistreated, and cast out. She knew what it felt like to be unwanted and pushed aside. She found herself in the wilderness, carrying pain, fear, and uncertainty about the future. She was a woman with wounds, and yet in the middle of her rejection, God saw her.

That is what touches my heart so deeply about Hagar's story. When others overlooked her, Heaven did not. When others cast her aside, God drew near. In the wilderness, where she may have felt forgotten by people, she was still fully seen by the Lord.

Hagar called Him **El Roi**, "the God who sees me."

Genesis 16:13 says, "And she called the name of the Lord who spoke unto her: "Thou God seest me." For she said, "Have I also here looked upon Him that seeth me?" What a powerful truth for every rejected woman.

You may feel unseen by people, but you are not unseen by God.
You may feel cast aside, but you are not cast away.
You may feel forgotten, but Heaven has not forgotten your name.

There are women reading these words who know exactly what rejection feels like. Perhaps you were rejected by a parent who did not nurture you the way you longed for. Perhaps you were rejected by a husband, by friends, by leaders, or by people who misunderstood your heart. Perhaps you gave your love and your loyalty, only to be repaid with betrayal, distance, or abandonment. Perhaps you were mocked for your faith, ignored for your kindness, or pushed aside when all you wanted was to belong.

I know what it feels like to be rejected by someone who should have welcomed me with love. The first time I visited my husband's mother's house, I felt rejection before I ever felt welcome. She did not even know me, yet one of the first things she said was that

Monroe's first wife was very beautiful. Her words pierced my heart and left me feeling unloved and unaccepted.

Then, a week before Monroe and I were to be married, she said something else that wounded me deeply. She said that the first wife should be the last wife. Those words brought such sadness to my heart that I even told Monroe I did not want to marry him, because I did not want a life filled with drama and pain.

Even after many years of marriage, there were still times when I felt unloved and rejected by her. That kind of pain is hard to explain, because it does not always come through shouting or open conflict. Sometimes it lives in the quiet sorrow of not being embraced, not being accepted, and not feeling at home in someone's heart.

But even in that pain, God was with me. He saw what others did not see. He knew the silent hurt I carried. He knew how deeply rejection can wound a woman, especially when all she wanted was love, peace, and acceptance. And through it all, I had to bring that pain to the Lord again and again. I had to let Him remind me that even if someone did not receive me, I was still fully received by Him.

Rejection can make a woman build walls around her heart. It can make her afraid to trust, afraid to love, afraid to be vulnerable, afraid to hope. It can whisper lies in the night and tell her that she is unwanted, unworthy, and unloved.

But rejection is a liar.

The truth is this: your worth was never meant to be decided by the people who wounded you. Your value does not rise, or fall based

on who accepted you or who walked away from you. Your identity
is not in who rejected you. Your identity is in the God who created
you, called you, and loves you with an everlasting love.

People may reject what they do not understand. They may walk
away from what they do not value. They may speak carelessly
about what God calls precious. But none of that changes what God
says about you.

You are seen.
You are known.
You are loved.
You are chosen.
You are not forgotten.

Sometimes God allows us to walk through rejection, not to destroy
us, but to free us from needing our identity to come from people.
That fire is painful, but it can also be holy. In that place, God
teaches us that His acceptance is deeper than human approval. His
love is steadier than human affection. His voice is truer than every
cruel word spoken over us.

The woman who feels rejected must learn to bring her pain to the
feet of Jesus. She must let Him touch the hidden places. She must
let Him heal the places where shame tried to settle. She must let
Him tear down the lies and rebuild her heart in truth.

This healing does not always happen in one day. Sometimes it is a
journey. Sometimes the tears return. Sometimes the memory still
hurts. But little by little, the love of God restores what rejection
tried to steal.

There are some wounds people never apologized for. There are some doors that are closed without explanation. There are some relationships that ended without the healing we hoped for. But even there, God remains faithful. He knows what was done to you. He knows what was said about you. He knows the tears you cried in private. And He is not indifferent to your pain.

The same God who found Hagar in the wilderness still meets women in lonely places today.

He sees the woman crying in secret.
He sees the woman trying to stay strong.
He sees the woman who wonders if anyone truly understands.
He sees the woman who feels left behind.
He sees the woman who has been talked about, cast aside, and deeply hurt.
He sees her, and He does not turn away.

Maybe rejection has been part of your story, but it does not have to become your identity.

You are not "the unwanted one."
You are not "the forgotten one."
You are not "the one nobody chose."
You are a daughter of the living God.

The Lord does not only see you in your rejection. He meets you there, speaks to you there, and begins to restore you there. The wilderness is not the end of your story. Sometimes it is the place where you first discover how near God really is.

I know that pain can leave deep marks on a woman's heart. I know rejection can make you feel voiceless, overlooked, and alone. But I also know this: God has a way of meeting wounded women with tender mercy. He does not despise the brokenhearted. He draws near to them.

If people have rejected you, let God remind you today that He has received you.
If people have misunderstood you, let God remind you that He knows your heart.
If people have cast you aside, let God remind you that you are still in His hands.

The woman who feels rejected is not abandoned by God.
She is seen.
She is loved.
She is carried.

And when God carries a woman through the fire of rejection, she comes out knowing something she may never have known any other way:

The God who sees her will never leave her.

Prayer

Lord,
For every woman who feels rejected, forgotten, overlooked, or abandoned, draw near to her today. Heal the wounds that people cannot see. Silence every lie that tells her she is unwanted or

unloved. Let her know deep in her heart that You are the God who sees her. Restore her identity, strengthen her spirit, and surround her with Your love. Where rejection has burned deeply, let Your healing flow even deeper. Remind her that she is chosen, treasured, and never alone.
In Jesus' name, amen.

Truth for the Woman in the Fire

Even if people rejected you, God still chose you.
Even if others did not see your value, Heaven does.
Even if you were cast aside, you are still held in the loving hands of God.

Chapter 2

The Woman Who Prays Through Tears

Some prayers are whispered with peace.
Some are spoken with joy.
And some are poured out through tears.

There are seasons in a woman's life when words do not come easily. The pain is too deep, the burden is too heavy, and the heart is too full. In those moments, prayer does not always sound polished or strong. Sometimes it trembles. Sometimes it breaks. Sometimes it comes through silent weeping in the presence of God.

But Heaven understands tears.

One of the most tender stories in Scripture is the story of **Hannah**. She was a woman who knew what it meant to carry deep sorrow. She longed for a child, yet year after year she lived with heartbreak, disappointment, and the pain of unanswered prayers. On top of that, she endured provocation and misunderstanding. Her grief was not light, and her tears were not small.

Yet Hannah did something beautiful in her pain: she brought it to the Lord.

She did not hide her sorrow from God. She did not pretend she was fine. She did not cover her brokenness with empty words. She poured out her soul before Him.

That is one of the most powerful things a woman can do.

There is something holy about a woman who still goes to God when her heart is breaking. There is something precious about tears that fall in prayer. The world may see them as weakness, but God sees them as trust. Every tear laid before Him becomes a kind of offering. Every cry in the night is heard by the One who never sleeps.

Many women know what it is to pray through tears.

Some pray through the tears of rejection.
Some through loneliness.
Some through grief.
Some through betrayal.
Some through fear for their children.
Some through marriage pain.
Some through waiting, disappointment, and long seasons of silence.

I know what it is to cry tears that came from deep heartbreak. One of the most painful seasons of my life was when my first husband, Joel, took my children from Germany to Athens, Georgia, in the United States. He had been unfaithful, and I had asked for a divorce. The German court had given me full custody of my two children, but without me knowing, he already had a plan.

That day, I cried with grief that felt impossible to describe. It was as though my heart was being taken from me piece by piece. The pain was so sharp, so heavy, and so unbearable that only God truly knew the depth of it. Those were not light tears. They were the tears of a mother whose heart was breaking.

In that kind of sorrow, words often fail. Some pain is too deep to explain to people. It can only be poured out before God. And when I had no strength left, when my heart felt shattered and helpless, I cried before the Lord. I believe He saw every tear, heard every cry, and stayed with me in that place of agony.

The woman who prays through tears may look strong on the outside while privately carrying a burden no one else can fully see. She may smile in public and weep in private. She may continue serving, loving, and showing up for others while quietly asking God, *Lord, do You see me? Do You hear me? How much longer?*

Hannah knew that place.

Scripture tells us that she was in bitterness of soul and prayed to the Lord and wept in anguish. What a description of deep pain. Yet even in that anguish, she turned toward God, not away from Him. Her tears became prayer. Her sorrow became surrender. Her brokenness became the very place where she encountered the heart of God.

That speaks deeply to me, because I believe many women have prayed prayers they could never fully explain to other people. Some burdens are too sacred for public words. Some heartbreaks are carried so deeply that only God truly knows the weight of them. But He does know. He knows every silent cry, every trembling prayer, every ache hidden behind tired eyes.

The woman who prays through tears is not forgotten.

She is seen by God in the late-night hours.
She is heard by God in the quiet places.
She is held by God in the middle of her breaking.

And sometimes, when others do not understand her grief, God understands it completely.

Hannah was even misunderstood by Eli at first. What a painful thing that must have been — to be carrying real sorrow and to be misjudged in the middle of it. Yet even that did not stop her from pouring out her heart before the Lord.

There may be women reading this chapter who know what that feels like too. You were genuinely hurting, but others did not understand. You were crying out to God, but someone misread your tears. You were fighting to stay faithful, but people only saw your outward emotion and not the deep place of prayer underneath it.

Beloved woman of God do not let misunderstanding keep you from the presence of the Lord.

Pray anyway.
Weep anyway.
Pour out your soul anyway.

God is not offended by your tears. He welcomes them.

Your tears do not make you weak. They reveal that your heart is still tender before the Lord. There are tears that come from self-pity, but there are also tears that come from deep longing, holy surrender, and aching faith. Hannah's tears were not empty emotion. They were the language of a soul reaching for God.

Sometimes the strongest prayer a woman can pray is the one she prays while crying.

Not because she has all the answers.
Not because everything makes sense.
But because somewhere in the middle of the tears, she still believes God is listening.

That is faith.

Faith is not always loud.
Sometimes faith kneels.
Sometimes faith trembles.
Sometimes faith cries.
Sometimes faith says, "Lord, I do not understand, but I am still here."

And that kind of faith is precious to God.

There are seasons when a woman grows weary in prayer. She has asked, waited, hoped, and cried for so long that her heart feels tired. She wonders if heaven is silent. She wonders if her tears matter. She wonders if the answer will ever come.

But Scripture reminds us that God stores our tears. He sees what others miss. He hears what others overlook. Not one tear shed in His presence is wasted.

Hannah's story reminds us that tears can water the ground where miracles grow.

What began in anguish ended in answered prayer.
What began in sorrow became a testimony.
What began in tears became worship.

This does not mean every answer comes in the exact way, or timing we expect. But it does mean that no woman who cries out to God is ever crying into emptiness. The Lord is near to the brokenhearted. He is attentive to the prayers, prayed in pain. He is gentle with women who come to Him undone.

I have learned that tears in prayer are not a sign that God has left us. Sometimes they are the very place where He meets us most tenderly. There are moments when words fail, but the heart still reaches upward. There are times when all we can do is sit before Him and cry. Yet even there, God is present. Even there, He is listening. Even there, He is working.

The woman who prays through tears is often a woman being formed in deep places. Her pain is teaching her to lean. Her sorrow is teaching her to trust. Her waiting is deepening her faith. And though the fire is painful, it is also holy, because it is drawing her closer to the heart of God.

Dear woman of God, if you have been praying through tears, do not lose heart.

Your tears are seen.
Your prayers are heard.
Your soul is held.

Keep coming to the Lord. Keep pouring out your heart. Keep trusting the God who understands what no one else can fully understand. Keep believing that the One who hears your weeping also holds your future.

And when God carries a woman through the fire of sorrow, she discovers this tender truth:

The tears she cried before Him were never wasted.

Prayer

Lord,
For every woman who has prayed through tears, draw near to her today. Meet her in the place of sorrow, disappointment, longing, and pain. Remind her that You see every tear and hear every prayer. Strengthen her when she feels weary. Hold her when she feels broken. Let Your peace rest upon her heart and let hope rise again within her. Teach her to trust You even in the waiting and surround her with Your tender love.
In Jesus' name, amen.

Truth for the Woman in the Fire

Your tears are not weakness.
They are prayers God understands.
The Lord hears every cry that is poured out before Him.

Chapter 3

The Woman Carrying Heavy Loss

Some losses happen suddenly.
Some unfold slowly.
Some can be seen by everyone.
And some are carried quietly in the deepest parts of a woman's heart.

Loss has a way of changing a woman. It can touch her home, her family, her future, her sense of safety, and even the way she sees herself. It can come through death, separation, betrayal, broken dreams, lost years, lost relationships, lost opportunities, or seasons that did not turn out the way she had prayed.

Heavy loss does not just wound the heart. It can leave a woman feeling emptied, shaken, and unsure how to keep walking forward.

One of the women in Scripture who knew heavy loss was **Ruth**.

Ruth's story is often remembered as beautiful, and it is. But before it became a story of redemption, it was a story marked by sorrow. Ruth lost her husband. Naomi lost her husband and her sons. Their lives were touched by grief, uncertainty, and the painful undoing of what once felt secure.

Before Ruth reached a field of provision, she walked through a valley of loss.

That is important to remember.

Sometimes when we read the beautiful ending of a Bible story, we forget the tears that came first. We forget that before restoration came, sorrow had already done its deep and painful work. Ruth was not walking through a light disappointment. She was carrying real loss. She had known love, and then she had known absence. She had known, belonging, and then she had known grief.

Many women understand that kind of pain.

There are women carrying losses no one else can fully measure. Some are grieving people they loved deeply. Some are carrying the pain of children far away, broken families, broken trust, broken marriages, shattered hopes, or years that seem stolen by suffering. Some are mourning not only what happened, but what never happened. Some are grieving dreams that died quietly in the waiting.

Heavy loss can make a woman feel as though something inside her has gone silent.

It can make ordinary days feel heavy.
It can make memories sting.
It can make the future feel uncertain.
It can make the heart ask, *"How do I go on from here?"*

Ruth knew what it meant to keep walking while carrying sorrow.

What touches me deeply about Ruth is that she did not have every answer, yet she kept going. She stayed faithful in grief. She kept walking through uncertainty. She remained loyal in a season that could have left her bitter, hopeless, and broken. There is something deeply beautiful about a woman who keeps walking with God even when life has stripped so much away.

Loss has a way of exposing what is fragile in us. It can bring us to the end of our own strength. It can uncover fears we did not know were there. It can leave us face-to-face with questions that do not have easy answers.

But it is often there, in that stripped-down place, that God begins to reveal Himself in deeper ways.

The woman carrying heavy loss may feel weak, but she is often stronger than she knows. She may not feel brave, but every step she takes in faith is courage. She may feel empty, but God is able to fill the places sorrow has hollowed out.

I know something about what it means to carry heavy loss.

I do not remember losing my father, because he went to heaven when I was only two years old. But even if my memory cannot hold that moment, my life still carries the absence of it. My mother was my world. She was the second wife of my father. He had been a widower and had six children, but I was the only child born to my mother. Losing her twenty-three years ago was one of the hardest losses I have ever carried.

I have also known the pain of losing others I loved. I lost a good friend when she was only sixteen years old. I still remember the sorrow of that. And the first time I can truly remember crying deeply over someone I lost was when my uncle died. He was kind to me, and I loved him very much. I was only six years old, but I still remember crying so hard at his funeral. That memory has never fully left me.

When losses come again and again, they can leave a deep ache in the heart. There were times I felt as though everyone who loved me was leaving me. That kind of sorrow can settle quietly into the soul. It can make the heart feel fragile. It can make love feel costly. It can make a woman wonder how much more loss she can bear.

But even in that pain, God has been with me. He has seen every funeral tear, every silent ache, and every memory that still hurts. He has stayed with me in the empty places. And little by little, He has reminded me that even when people I loved were taken from this earth, I was never abandoned by Him.

Yet even there, God remains faithful.

He is faithful in the empty places.
He is faithful in the grieving places.
He is faithful in the places where tears come without warning.

Ruth's story reminds us that loss is not the end of the story.

Yes, she lost.
Yes, she grieved.
Yes, she walked through uncertainty.
But God was already writing redemption in places she could not yet see.

That is one of the tender mercies of God: while we are grieving what has been lost, He is still at work in what remains. While we are mourning what has ended, He is still guarding what is ahead. While we are carrying sorrow, He is still carrying us.

Heavy loss can tempt a woman to believe that her best days are over. It can whisper that nothing beautiful can come again. It can tell her that because something precious was lost, her life will forever remain only a story of pain.

But God writes differently.

He knows how to bring beauty into broken places.
He knows how to bring provision into empty seasons.
He knows how to bring tenderness into wounded hearts.
He knows how to lead a grieving woman one step at a time.

This does not mean loss is small. It is not small. Grief is real. The ache is real. The empty places are real. God does not ask us to pretend otherwise. He is not honored by false strength. He welcomes the honest heart. He welcomes the tears. He welcomes the weary soul that comes to Him and says, "Lord, I do not know how to carry this."

And that is where His grace begins to hold us.

The woman carrying heavy loss does not need to have everything figured out. She only needs to keep bringing her sorrow to the One who understands it completely. She only needs to keep walking, even if it's slow. She only needs to trust that the God who met Ruth in her grief still meets women in grief today.

Maybe you are carrying a loss that no one else fully understands.

Maybe you are grieving a person.
Maybe you are grieving your family as it once was.
Maybe you are grieving the life you thought you would have.
Maybe you are grieving years that feel stolen.
Maybe you are carrying sorrow so deeply that words still fail.

Beloved woman of God, the Lord sees the weight you carry.

He sees the brave face.
He sees the tired heart.
He sees the memories that still hurt.
He sees the questions you cannot answer.
He sees the strength it takes just to keep going.

And He is near.

The same God who guided Ruth through loss will guide you. The same God who provided for Ruth will provide for you. The same God who turned grief into a testimony is still able to write redemption in your life.

Perhaps not all at once.
Perhaps not in the way you expected.
But faithfully, tenderly, and one day at a time.

When God carries a woman through the fire of heavy loss, He does not waste her tears. He does not despise her weakness. He does not abandon her, in her emptiness. He walks with her until sorrow no longer has the final word.

And in time, she begins to discover a truth that grief could not erase:

What was lost was real, but so is the God who remained.

Prayer

Lord,
For every woman carrying heavy loss, draw near to her today.
Hold the places in her heart that still ache. Comfort her in the grief
she cannot put into words. Strengthen her when she feels weak and
remind her that she does not carry this sorrow alone. Just as You
walked with Ruth through grief and uncertainty, walk with her
now. Bring peace where there is heaviness, hope where there is
sorrow, and gentle healing where the pain has settled deeply.
In Jesus' name, amen.

Truth for the Woman in the Fire

God sees the weight you carry.
God stays with you in your grief.
And even in loss, God is still writing redemption.

Chapter 4

The Woman Called to Stand Courageously

There are moments in a woman's life when she must choose whether she will shrink back in fear or stand in faith.

Courage does not always feel strong. It does not always look fearless. Sometimes courage is trembling hands, a breaking heart, and a quiet prayer whispered before taking the next step. Sometimes courage is simply obeying God when the cost feels high and the outcome is uncertain.

One of the women in Scripture who shows us this kind of courage is **Esther**.

Esther did not begin her story as a woman standing boldly before a king. She began as a young woman carrying her own hidden pain. She was an orphan. She knew what it meant to lose. She knew what it meant to be placed in circumstances she did not choose. Yet in the middle of her story, God positioned her for something greater than she could have imagined.

When the time came, Esther was faced with a moment that required courage. Her people were in danger. The threat was real. The risk was great. And to step forward could cost her everything.

That is what makes her story so powerful.

Esther did not step forward because it was easy.
She stepped forward because it was necessary.
She stepped forward because silence was no longer an option.
She stepped forward because purpose was calling louder than fear.

How many women have stood in that same kind of moment?

There are women who have had to stand courageously in marriage.
Women who have had to stand for their children.
Women who have had to stand in the face of injustice.
Women who have had to stand after betrayal, after pain, after loss,
and after being underestimated.
Women who have had to speak truth with tears in their eyes and
faith in their hearts.

To stand courageously does not mean you feel no fear. Esther
surely felt fear. She understood the danger. She knew what she was
risking. *But courage is not the absence of fear.* Courage is choosing
obedience even when fear is present.

That is what makes holy courage so beautiful. It is not rooted in
self-confidence. It is rooted in surrender to God.

Esther did not rush ahead with her own strength. She called for
fasting. She recognized that what she was facing required more
than human bravery. It required the help of God. Before she
stepped into the public moment, she first went into a private place
of consecration.

There is deep wisdom in that.

The courageous woman is not merely bold.
She is prayerful.
She is surrendered.
She is strengthened by the Lord before she steps into the fire.

Many women are asked to stand in hard places.

Some are called to stand when they are misunderstood.
Some are called to stand when they are opposed.
Some are called to stand when their voice shakes.
Some are called to stand when no one else around them
understands why it matters so much.

And sometimes, standing courageously means standing alone for a
while.

That can be one of the hardest fires of all.

It is not easy to stand when people question you.
It is not easy to stand when others want you to stay quiet.
It is not easy to stand when you know your obedience may cost
you comfort, approval, or peace with people.

But there are moments when a woman must remember that
pleasing God matters more than pleasing people.

Esther's words still echo through time:

"If I perish, I perish."

What a statement of surrender.
What a statement of courage.
What a statement of trust.

She was saying, in essence, *I will obey God, no matter the cost.*

That kind of courage does not come from personality. It comes from a heart that has yielded itself to the Lord.

I believe many women carry courage they do not even realize they have until the fire comes. Sometimes we do not know the strength God has placed within us until life demands that we stand. Sometimes we discover our courage only when we have no choice but to trust Him.

There have been seasons in my own life when I had to stand through pain, through sorrow, and through things I never would have chosen. One of the deepest examples of that was when I stood in court to testify after being sold into human trafficking while I was still underage. I had been sold for fifteen thousand Deutsche Mark. What was done to me was evil, painful, and deeply wrong. I was not being helped as I had been led to believe. I was being used for someone else's profit.

A few years later, I stood in court and testified to the truth. I told the court that Emma Romeo and her husband, Alexander Romeo, were not helping women find work. They were selling women for their own profit. They would bring women two by two so the German authorities would not notice that what they were doing was illegal.

Standing there and speaking the truth was not easy. It took courage to face what had happened and to testify about it. But by the grace of God, I stood. And in the end, both of them went to prison.

Looking back, I know that was not my strength alone. God gave me courage to speak. God gave me strength to stand. God gave me grace to face evil with truth. What the enemy meant for harm did not have the final word. God was with me, and justice was done.

There are times when a woman does not feel strong at all, yet the grace of God helps her keep standing. That is one of the miracles of His strength. He gives courage that is greater than our natural ability. He steadies us when our hearts are trembling. He helps us remain faithful when the fire is intense.

The woman called to stand courageously may feel small, but she is not powerless.

She is backed by heaven.
She is strengthened by grace.
She is upheld by the hand of God.

Sometimes courage means speaking.
Sometimes courage means waiting.
Sometimes courage means walking away from what is wrong.
Sometimes courage means stepping into what is right, even if it is costly.

Whatever form it takes, courage becomes holy when it is offered back to God in obedience.

Beloved woman of God, perhaps you are standing in a hard place right now. Perhaps the Lord is asking you to trust Him in a way that stretches you. Perhaps you feel the weight of responsibility, the burden of speaking truth, or the pressure of making a difficult decision.

Take heart.

The same God who strengthened Esther will strengthen you.
The same God who positioned Esther has positioned you.
The same God who gave her favor, wisdom, and courage will not fail you now.

You do not have to stand in your own strength.
You do not have to create courage by yourself.
You do not have to pretend you are not afraid.

Bring your fear to God.
Bring your weakness to God.
Bring your questions to God.

Then rise in the strength He supplies.

The woman called to stand courageously is not always the loudest woman in the room. She is the woman who has met with God and decided that obedience matters more than fear.

And when God carries a woman through the fire of courage, she learns something powerful:

She was never standing alone.

Prayer

Lord,
For every woman You are calling to stand courageously, strengthen her today. When fear rises, fills her with faith. When her heart trembles, steady her with Your peace. Give her wisdom, boldness, and grace for every step she must take. Help her to trust You more than she fears people, more than she fears outcomes, and more than she fears the unknown. Remind her that if You have called her, You will also sustain her.
In Jesus' name, amen.

Truth for the Woman in the Fire

Courage does not mean you feel no fear.
Courage means you trust God enough to obey anyway.
When God calls you to stand, He will also give you strength.

Chapter 5

The Woman Who Suffers in Silence

Not all pain is loud.

Some suffering is hidden behind a smile.
Some sorrow is tucked beneath daily responsibilities.
Some wounds are carried so quietly that no one knows how much a woman is truly enduring.

There are women who keep going while privately bleeding.
They show up.
They serve.
They care for others.
They keep moving through life while carrying pain they do not always have words for.

This is the kind of sorrow that often lives in silence.

One of the most tender and powerful stories in Scripture is the story of **the woman with the issue of blood**. For twelve long years, she suffered. Twelve years is not a short trial. It is not a passing storm. It is a long season of pain, weakness, disappointment, and endurance. Her suffering affected her body, her daily life, and her place among others. She knew what it was to carry a burden that did not quickly leave.

What touches my heart is that much of her suffering was hidden in plain sight. Many people may have seen her, but very few truly understood her pain. That is often the way silent suffering works. People may see the woman, but they do not see the depth of what she has been carrying.

And yet Jesus saw her.

That changes everything.

There are women who suffer in silence through physical pain.
Some through emotional wounds.
Some through rejection.
Some through fear and anxiety.
Some through private grief.
Some through memories they do not know how to explain.
Some through seasons of shame, loneliness, or being deeply misunderstood.

The woman who suffers in silence often learns how to function while hurting. She becomes skilled at carrying pain without showing all of it. She may not want to burden others. She may feel that no one would understand. She may even believe she has to endure it quietly because there is no place safe enough to fully lay it down.

But silent suffering still matters to God.

The woman with the issue of blood did not stop reaching for Jesus because her pain had gone on so long. She did not say, "It has been too many years," or "Nothing will ever change," or "Perhaps this is just how my life will always be." Somehow, in the middle of her suffering, faith still reached forward.

That is what makes her story so beautiful.

She was weak, yet she reached.
She was hurting, yet she reached.
She had suffered for a long time, yet she reached.

Sometimes that is what faith looks like.

Not loud preaching.
Not great strength.
Not having it all together.

Sometimes faith is simply reaching for Jesus while still bleeding.

I believe many women understand that kind of reaching. They know what it is to wake up with pain and still whisper a prayer. They know what it is to keep trusting God while carrying something no one else can fully see. They know what it is to hope quietly, to endure quietly, and to cry quietly.

I know something about that too.

In **March 2010**, I was in a car accident. I was stopped at a traffic light, getting ready to turn right, when someone hit the back of my car. The driver had been texting and was not paying attention. After that accident, my body began to change in painful ways. I started having severe nerve pain in my legs, arms, and hands. There were shooting pains through my body, and even simple things became difficult. At times, I could not even hold a bottle of water. My neck hurt so badly that in **May 2010**, I had neck surgery at **C5-C6**.

Even after the surgery, the pain did not fully leave. My nerves still hurt, and my memory started getting worse. The doctors called the nerve damage **fibromyalgia**. That was a hard season for me, because I had always remembered Scripture so easily. Before, I could recall the Word of God as if it were the back of my hand. So, I began to pray and ask the Lord to help me day by day. And one of the deepest cries of my heart was this: **"Lord, please do not take Your Word from my memory. How can I tell people the good news of the gospel if I cannot remember Your Word?"**

God was so good to me. He brought His Word back to me. And though my body has continued to go through pain, I remain thankful to Him. As long as God helps me walk through each day, I will thank Him. His grace has been with me in the pain, and His faithfulness has carried me through what others could not fully see.

There are seasons in life when a woman carries pain so deeply that not everyone around her sees it. The heart can be breaking while the face still smiles. The soul can be weary while the body keeps moving. Silent suffering has a way of teaching a woman how to endure, but it can also make her feel alone if she does not remember that God sees what people miss.

There are burdens that are hard to explain. There are wounds that do not always show on the outside. There are sorrows that stay hidden in the secret places of the heart. And yet none of it is hidden from God.

Jesus did not ignore that woman in the crowd. He felt her touch.
He noticed her faith. He stopped for her.

What tenderness.
What mercy.
What attention, from the Savior.

In a crowd full of people, Jesus still stopped for one suffering
woman.

That truth is deeply comforting to me. It reminds me that the Lord
does not overlook the woman who has been quietly carrying pain
for a long time. He does not ignore her because others do not
notice. He does not pass by because her suffering is hidden. He sees
her reaching, and He responds with compassion.

The woman with the issue of blood had likely known
disappointment after disappointment. She had suffered for years.
She had tried. She had waited. She had endured. Yet when she
touched Jesus, everything changed.

Sometimes a woman has been silent for so long that she begins to
believe her suffering no longer matters. She may begin to think her
pain is too old, too complicated, or too invisible. She may tell
herself to just keep going, to not speak of it, to keep it buried.

But Jesus is not intimidated by long pain.

He is not weary of wounds that have lasted years.
He is not distant from hidden sorrow.
He is not unmoved by silent tears.

He is still the Healer.
He is still the One who stops.
He is still the One who calls suffering women **daughter**.

What a beautiful word that is.

Not problem.
Not burden.
Not interruption.

Daughter.

That means tenderness.
That means belonging.
That means love.
That means she was not forgotten in her suffering.

Beloved woman of God, perhaps you are carrying something quietly right now. Perhaps you have suffered longer than anyone realizes. Perhaps you are tired of explaining. Perhaps you are tired of hoping. Perhaps you are weary from appearing strong while hurting underneath it all.

Please hear this truth:

Jesus sees your silent suffering.
Jesus honors your reach of faith.
Jesus has not forgotten you.

You may be one touch away from a holy moment.
You may be one prayer away from fresh strength.
You may be closer to His healing presence than you realize.

The woman who suffers in silence does not have to remain unseen forever. The Lord who stopped in the middle of a crowd is still the Lord who stops for hurting women today.

He sees the hidden tears.
He sees the sleepless nights.
He sees the old wounds.
He sees the burden you have not fully spoken aloud.

And He does not turn away.

When God carries a woman through the fire of silent suffering, she begins to learn that even what was hidden from others was never hidden from Him.

And in that holy place, she discovers this tender truth:

Jesus still stops for the woman who reaches for Him in secret.

Prayer

Lord,
For every woman who suffers in silence, draw near to her today. See the pain she has hidden, the tears she has swallowed, and the burdens she has carried alone. Let her feel Your nearness in the secret places of her heart. Strengthen her faith to keep reaching for You. Bring healing where there is pain, peace where there is unrest, and comfort where there has been silent sorrow for too long.
Remind her that she is not invisible to You.
In Jesus' name, amen.

Truth for the Woman in the Fire

Your pain is not hidden from God.
Your quiet faith still reaches His heart.
Jesus still stops for the woman who reaches for Him.

Chapter 6

The Woman Bound by the Past

Some women are not only fighting what is happening now. They are also carrying what happened before.

The past can be a heavy chain. It can follow a woman into new seasons, whispering old names, old fears, old shame, and old pain. It can remind her of what was done to her, what was said about her, what she lost, what she survived, and what she wishes had never happened.

Even after life moves forward, the heart can still feel tied to yesterday.

That is why this fire is so deep.

A woman bound by the past may look fine on the outside, yet inwardly she is still wrestling with old wounds. She may still hear the voices that once condemned her. She may still feel the weight of things she has suffered. She may still struggle to believe she is truly free, truly clean, truly loved, and truly made new.

One of the women in Scripture who reminds us of the redeeming power of Jesus is **Mary Magdalene**.

Mary Magdalene is remembered as a woman deeply touched by the power of God. Jesus delivered her, and from that moment on, her life was never the same. She became a woman marked not by what had once bound her, but by the One who had set her free.

That is what makes her story so powerful.

She had a past.
She had known darkness.
She had known bondage.
But her past was not stronger than the power of Jesus.

What a message of hope for every woman carrying memories she cannot erase.

There are women bound by the past in many ways.

Some are bound by abuse.
Some by betrayal.
Some by shame.
Some by guilt.
Some by trauma.
Some by words spoken over them long ago.
Some by sins they committed.
Some by wounds they did not deserve.
Some by things they survived but still struggle to speak about.

The past has a cruel way of trying to become an identity. It tells a woman that because something happened to her, she will always be defined by it. It tells her she will never fully heal, never fully trust, never fully rise, never fully belong.

But Jesus speaks a better word.

The woman bound by the past needs to know this: what happened to you is not the whole story of who you are. What broke you is not your final name. What tried to bury you is not the end God has written over your life.

Mary Magdalene could have remained known only for what once held her captive. But instead, she became known for her devotion to Jesus. She stood near Him. She followed Him faithfully. She was present in grief. She was present in love. And she was one of the first to witness the risen Christ.

What a redemption story.

The woman who had once known bondage became a woman trusted with good news.

That speaks so deeply to my heart.

Jesus does not merely forgive a woman and leave her in chains. He restores her. He gives her dignity. He gives her new identity. He gives her a future that is no longer ruled by the darkness behind her.

I know something about what it means to carry a painful past.

For a long time, I carried shame about what had happened to me when I was sold. I felt as though it was my fault, even though it was not. Because of that shame, I did not tell many people about my past. I kept much of it hidden deep inside.

Years later, there was a man who worked for us as a handyman. I called him Papa Richard. He was probably around sixty-five or older. I began to notice that when my husband was working the night shift, he would come to the property where we had been working and talk with me. One evening, knowing my husband would not be there, he came inside the property and sat down in one of the chairs. Then he pulled me onto his lap and kissed my cheek.

I stood up right away and told him that what he had done was not right. I told him to get out of the house.

What happened stirred something painful inside me. It touched places in my heart that already knew what it felt like to be violated, shamed, and wounded. For a moment, it tried to make me feel as though it was somehow my fault again. But God began to speak truth to my heart: **It was not my fault.** It was not my fault when I was sold, and it was not my fault that this man had wrong intentions toward women.

Later, I found out that he had done something similar to another woman in the church. When I called a woman who knew him from another church, the first thing she asked me was, "What did Richard do to you?" She then told me what he had done to another woman.

I prayed about the situation and asked God what He wanted me to do. Then, by His strength, I brought the man to court and testified about what he had done. What the enemy thought would keep me silent, God turned for good. The Lord gave me boldness to speak out. He reminded me that shame did not belong to me. Truth belonged to me. Courage belonged to me through Him.

There are some things a woman lives through that do not leave easily. Some experiences mark the soul so deeply that even after time passes, the memory still aches. There are seasons when the past tries to speak louder than the present. It tries to remind you of what was stolen, what was broken, what was done, and what can never be undone.

And yet, I have learned this: the healing power of Jesus is greater than the grip of the past.

The Lord knows how to step into the places we do not know how to fix. He knows how to touch what is wounded, lift what is bowed down, and restore what shame tried to bury. He knows how to break chains we thought would follow us forever.

This does not mean the past never hurts again. Some memories still sting. Some scars remain tender. Some chapters can still bring tears. But healing means the past no longer rules you. It no longer names you. It no longer owns your future.

That is freedom.

Freedom is not pretending nothing happened.
Freedom is knowing that what happened no longer has the right to define you.

The woman bound by the past often needs time to believe she is truly free. She may love God and still wrestle with old pain. She may know truth in her mind while still healing in her heart. She may need the Lord to remind her again and again that she is not who she once was, and she is not what others did to her.

Beloved woman of God, if your past still tries to follow you, hear this tender truth:

Jesus is not afraid of your history.
He is not ashamed of your wounds.
He is not overwhelmed by what you survived.

He sees it all, and He still calls you forward.

He still calls you daughter.
He still calls you loved.
He still calls you redeemed.
He still calls you His own.

The enemy wants a woman to live looking backward, trapped in regret, shame, fear, or pain. But Jesus calls her out of the shadows and into His marvelous light. He does not erase the truth of what happened, but He transforms the meaning of it. What once looked like ruin can become testimony. What once looked like shame can become a story of grace. What once looked like the end can become the place where resurrection begins.

Mary Magdalene reminds us that deliverance is real. Restoration is real. A new beginning is real.

The same Jesus who set her free still breaks chains today.

Perhaps you have lived through things that still try to cling to you. Perhaps the past still speaks in moments of weakness. Perhaps there are memories that rise when you least expect them. Perhaps you wonder if you will ever fully walk in freedom.

Take heart.

The Lord is patient with the healing journey. He is gentle with wounded women. He does not crush bruised hearts. He restores them. He walks with us until the chain grows weaker, the wound grows cleaner, and the heart begins to believe again that freedom is truly possible.

When God carries a woman through the fire of her past, He does not leave her there. He leads her into a new place — a place of healing, identity, dignity, and hope.

And there, she begins to discover this beautiful truth:

Her past may explain part of her story, but it no longer owns her future.

Prayer

Lord,
For every woman who feels bound by her past, draw near to her today. Touch the places in her heart that still ache with memory, shame, fear, or sorrow. Break every chain that still tries to hold her. Speak louder than every lie from yesterday. Remind her that she is not abandoned, not ruined, and not beyond Your healing. Restore her dignity, renew her mind, and help her walk in the freedom You died to give her.
In Jesus' name, amen.

Truth for the Woman in the Fire

What happened to you is not your identity.
What once bound you is not stronger than Jesus.
Your past may be part of your story, but it is not your final name.

Chapter 7

The Woman Who Feels Too Weak

to Keep Going

There are seasons in a woman's life when she feels as though she has nothing left.

No strength.
No answers.
No energy.
No words.

Only weariness.

Sometimes the weariness is physical.
Sometimes it is emotional.
Sometimes it is spiritual.
And sometimes it is all three at once.

A woman can love God deeply and still feel exhausted. She can still pray and still feel tired. She can still believe and still feel as though her heart is barely holding on. There are moments when the burdens become so heavy, the battles so long, and the disappointments so deep that she quietly wonders, *Lord, how do I keep going from here?*

This is one of the hidden fires many women walk through.

It is the fire of depletion.
The fire of fatigue.
The fire of carrying too much for too long.

And yet, even there, God is near.

The woman who feels too weak to keep going may think her weakness is failure, but often it is simply proof that she has been carrying more than anyone knows. She has been standing through pain, loving through disappointment, praying through sorrow, and enduring through fires that would have made many others stop.

Sometimes weakness is not a sign that a woman has lost her faith. Sometimes it is a sign that she has been fighting for a very long time.

There are women who keep showing up while inwardly feeling worn thin.
They care for others while neglecting their own pain.
They keep serving, keep giving, keep pressing on, even when they feel as though their strength is running out.

To everyone else, they may look strong.
But in private, they whisper, *Lord, I am tired.*

What tenderness there is in knowing that God does not despise that prayer.

He is not disappointed by your weakness.
He is not irritated by your weariness.
He is not standing far away waiting for you to be stronger.

He draws near to the weary.

Scripture reminds us again and again that God gives strength to the faint. He renews those who wait on Him. He carries what we cannot carry alone. The Lord has never asked us to be self-sufficient. He has asked us to remain dependent on Him.

That is why weakness, though painful, can become a holy place.

It is the place where pride falls away.
It is the place where striving loses its grip.
It is the place where a woman learns that the grace of God really is enough.

So often, women think they must keep everything together. They must be strong for everyone. They must hold the family together, keep their faith steady, keep their home running, keep their smile in place, and keep their pain hidden. But the Lord never asked His daughters to live by human strength alone.

He says, in essence, *Come to Me. Bring Me your burden. Bring Me your weakness. Bring Me your tired heart.*

That invitation is mercy.

The woman who feels too weak to keep going does not need a lecture. She needs the gentle presence of God. She needs to know that even if she cannot run, she can still lean. Even if she cannot fix everything, she can still trust. Even if she cannot see the full road ahead, she can still take the next step with the Lord beside her.

I know something about that kind of weakness.

After my divorce, I gave my time to the Lord. I wanted to serve Him, study His Word, and know my Savior Jesus Christ more deeply. I worked at Blockbuster from Monday through Thursday so I could have health insurance, and on Friday, Saturday, and Sunday I ran my small business at the flea market. On Sunday mornings I went to Fleming Baptist Church, and after church I went to my store. In that season, I wanted it to be just me and God.

But even when a woman loves the Lord deeply, there can still be moments of deep loneliness. One Christmas, I was by myself because I wanted my children to be with their grandmother for the year. I did not want to take that from them. But that day, the sadness felt heavy, and I cried out to God. I said, **"Lord, You know my heart. I want it to be just You and me, but sometimes I just want someone to hold me and talk to me."**

A few months later, God brought Monroe into my life. Two of his friends, who did not know each other, had tried to bring us together in two separate years. First, Daniel, his coworker, mentioned me to Monroe. Then, the following year, Jeff, his best friend since childhood, also told Monroe about me. Looking back, I can see the kindness of God even in that lonely season. He heard the cry of my heart.

But there were other times in my life when my weakness felt even deeper than loneliness. One of those times was when I was in Germany, in the house of the mother who had bought me for her son Peter. In that place, I felt so hopeless. Another time was when my first husband, Joel, took my children and brought them to America. In those moments, the pain was so heavy that I felt as though my strength had run out completely.

Yet even there, God did not let me go. When I felt weakest, He kept me. When I felt empty, He sustained me. When I thought I could not go on, His grace carried me one step at a time. I have learned that weakness does not mean God has abandoned us. Sometimes weakness becomes the very place where His strength holds us most tenderly.

There is a quiet kind of miracle in daily strength.

Not always the strength to leap.
Not always the strength to conquer in one moment.
But the strength to rise again.
The strength to endure.
The strength to keep believing.
The strength to keep breathing hope into another day.

That kind of strength is sacred.

The woman who feels too weak to keep going often thinks she is failing when, in truth, she is being carried. She may not feel victorious. She may not feel brave. She may not feel powerful. But if she is still turning toward God, still whispering His name, still reaching for His help, then grace is already at work in her life.

Beloved woman of God, perhaps this is where you are.

Perhaps you are tired in ways no one sees.
Perhaps your mind is weary.
Perhaps your body is worn.
Perhaps your heart feels bruised from carrying too much for too long.

Please hear this:

God sees your weakness, and He is not ashamed of you.
God sees your weariness, and He is not turning away.
God sees how hard it has been, and He is still holding you.

You do not have to pretend to be stronger than you are.
You do not have to hide your need from God.
You do not have to prove anything to Heaven.

You are allowed to come weak.
You are allowed to come tired.
You are allowed to come with trembling hands and a weary soul.

And the Lord, in His tenderness, will still receive you.

Sometimes we think strength means never breaking down. But in the kingdom of God, strength often looks different. Sometimes strength looks like crying and still praying. Sometimes strength looks like resting in the arms of God when you have no energy left to stand on your own.

The Lord knows how to sustain a weary woman.

He knows how to breathe peace into a tired mind.
He knows how to pour comfort into a weary heart.
He knows how to strengthen hands that are hanging down.

And when He does, the woman who once thought she could not go on finds herself still standing — not because she was strong in herself, but because the everlasting arms of God were underneath her all along.

When God carries a woman through the fire of weakness, she learns a beautiful and humbling truth:

His strength is most visible where hers runs out.

Prayer

Lord,
For every woman who feels too weak to keep going, draw near to her today. Strengthen her where she is weary, comfort her where she is hurting, and hold her where she feels like she cannot take another step. Remind her that Your grace is sufficient and Your strength is made perfect in weakness. Teach her to rest in You, lean on You, and trust You one day at a time.
In Jesus' name, amen.

Truth for the Woman in the Fire

Your weakness does not disqualify you.
It is a place where God can meet you deeply.
When your strength runs out, His does not.

Chapter 8

The Woman God Is Refining

Refining is not a gentle word.

It speaks of fire.
It speaks of heat.
It speaks of a process that is not easy, quick, or comfortable.

And yet, in the hands of God, refining is never meant to destroy His daughters. It is meant to purify, strengthen, deepen, and prepare them for what He has called them to become.

The woman God is refining may not understand everything she is walking through. She may ask why the road has been so hard, why the fire has lasted so long, or why certain prayers seem delayed. She may wonder why the Lord allows such deep stretching, such painful shaping, and such intense seasons of testing.

But refining has purpose.

God does not waste pain.
He does not waste waiting.
He does not waste fire.

He uses it.

The woman God is refining is often a woman He loves deeply and is preparing carefully. He sees not only who she is now, but who she is becoming. He sees the strength He is building in her, the wisdom He is forming in her, the humility He is deepening in her, and the faith He is anchoring in her soul.

That does not mean the process feels easy.

Refining can look like being misunderstood.
It can look like losing what once felt secure.
It can look like walking through long trials.
It can look like prayers prayed with tears.
It can look like being stripped of self-reliance until all that is left is dependence on God.

And that can be painful.

But pain in God's hands is never pointless.

Gold is refined by fire, not because it is worthless, but because it is precious. The fire does not mean the gold has been rejected. It means it is being purified. In the same way, when God refines a woman, it is not because He has abandoned her. It is because He is doing a holy work in her that cannot be accomplished in comfort alone.

The woman God is refining may feel pressed, but she is not forgotten.
She may feel stretched, but she is still held.
She may feel broken in places, but she is not being ruined.

She is being made more like Christ.

That is the deepest purpose of refining.

Not merely to make a woman stronger in herself,
but to make her more surrendered, more holy, more
compassionate, more discerning, more prayerful, and more
anchored in the heart of God.

There are things we learn in the fire that we do not learn anywhere
else.

In the fire, we learn that God is enough.
In the fire, we learn that His presence is more precious than ease.
In the fire, we learn that our faith can survive more than we
thought.
In the fire, we learn that what God is building in us matters more
than what we are losing around us.

I know something about the refining hand of God.

When God refines us through fire, I believe it is a process of
spiritual purification and growth that takes place through life's
challenges and trials, much like metal is refined through intense
heat. As I look back on my life now, I can see how God used the
things I went through from the time I was young to shape me into
the woman I am today. Even from a young age, I believed God had
chosen me for His purpose. I believed He had called me to be a
worker for Him.

My refining began early.

As a child, I went through pain that no child should have to carry.
My cousins bullied me. There were times when they would not

give me food, and I had to beg for something to eat. When I was seven years old, there were times when I had no place to sleep, and I slept on the sidewalk. I was homeless twice.

Yet even in those early years, God was planting something in me. No one taught me how to do it, but when I was seven years old, I started my own little business. After school, Monday through Friday, I sold newspapers. I remember saving my extra coins, and on the weekends, I sold plastic bags. Even as a little girl, I was learning how to survive. I was learning how to keep going.

As I grew older, the fires continued. I was sold into human trafficking when I was sixteen years old. Later, my first husband took my children, and that was one of the deepest pains I had ever known. I also faced rejection in many different forms. My first mother-in-law once said that if I had been too dark, she would not have brought me into the house. Monroe's mother made me feel rejected and unwelcome in her home.

There were also people in church who hurt me. Some people expect the deepest kindness there, but sadly, even in places where God is worshiped, people can still wound one another. I remember one woman who was very nice to me at first, but when she realized I knew a lot about the Lord, her attitude changed. It felt as though she saw everything as a competition. But to me, serving God is not a competition. We are meant to work together for the Lord, not strive against one another.

I also remember being bullied in school because after school in high school, I sold fruit in the street. Some of my classmates and batchmates would not even talk to me because they were embarrassed. But I was not embarrassed. I was not doing anything wrong. I was trying to survive.

Through all of it, I can now see that God was giving me strength.

The fires were painful.
The pruning was painful.
The refining was painful.

There were many tears, much rejection, and many moments of feeling unloved, unseen, and unwanted. Sometimes the deepest bruises are not the ones people can see on the outside, but the ones left by harsh words, cruelty, and rejection.

But by the grace of God, I forgave them.

I forgave the people who hurt me when I was a child. I forgave those who rejected me. I forgave those who bullied me, even in church. I forgave because I know what it means to be forgiven by God. And I have learned that bitterness hardens a person, but forgiveness keeps the heart free.

I have also learned that the Bible does not say the *work* of your testimony. It says the **word of your testimony**. We testify so others can know how good God is. We speak so others can see that God brings His children through the fire. We tell what He has done so others will not lose hope in the middle of their own trials.

The Word of God says in **Revelation 12:11**, *"And they overcame him by the blood of the Lamb, and by the **word of their testimony**; and they loved not their lives unto the death."*

That verse means so much to me. It reminds me that testimony matters. It reminds me that what we have walked through is not wasted. God can use our pain, our tears, and our story to bring courage and hope to someone else.

So yes, refining hurts. Pruning hurts. Fire hurts. But God uses it to make us more like gold. He uses it to purify us, to strengthen us, and to prepare us.

Today, I can look back and see that everything I went through did not destroy me. By the grace of God, it made me stronger. It made me lean on Him. It made me trust Him. It made me more determined to love people, to be kind, and to tell others about Jesus.

I believe we should be kind whether we are inside the church or outside the church. We should not be bullies. We should not be jealous. We should not tear people down. If someone is beautiful, I can say, "You are beautiful." If someone smells nice, I can say, "You smell nice." I am not ashamed to encourage others. I believe we should lift one another up, not compete with one another.

My prayer is that this book will bless women who have gone through trials and tribulations. I pray they will know more about the Lord and will not lose heart because of what they have suffered. Jesus told us we would carry our cross, but He also told us to be of good cheer, because He has overcome the world.

And because He overcame, I believe we can overcome too.

The Lord is too loving to leave His daughters untouched by His refining work. He knows what must be burned away so that what is pure can shine more clearly. He knows what weights must fall off so that a woman can walk more freely in her calling. He knows what distractions must fade so that her heart can become wholly His.

The woman God is refining often feels alone in the process, but she is not alone. The Refiner never leaves the fire unattended. He watches over the process with care. He knows exactly how much heat is needed, exactly how long it must last, and exactly what He is producing through it.

That truth is deeply comforting.

The fire is not random.
The trial is not wasted.
The stretching is not meaningless.

God sees the end from the beginning.

Beloved woman of God, perhaps you are in a refining season right now.

Perhaps you feel the heat of trial.
Perhaps you feel stripped down.
Perhaps you feel tired of being shaped through hardship.
Perhaps you wonder if anything beautiful could come from all this pain.

Yes, beautiful things can come from the fire.

Purity can come.
Wisdom can come.

Depth can come.
Compassion can come.
Strength can come.
A closer walk with God can come.

The Lord knows what He is doing in you.

You may not yet see all of it.
You may not yet understand all of it.
But one day you will look back and see that the fire did not
consume you.

It refined you.

It taught you to pray more deeply.
It taught you to trust more fully.
It taught you to cling to Jesus more closely.
It taught you that even in the hardest places, God was still forming
something beautiful in you.

When God carries a woman through the fire of refining, she comes
out with a deeper faith, a purer heart, and a stronger awareness of
His presence.

And in time, she begins to understand this holy truth:

**The fire did not come to destroy her. It came to reveal the work of
God within her.**

Prayer

Lord,
For every woman walking through a refining season, strengthen her today. When the fire feels intense, remind her that You have not left her. When the process feels long, help her trust Your wisdom. Purify what needs to be purified, heal what needs to be healed, and shape her into the woman You have called her to be. Let the fire draw her closer to You, not farther away.
In Jesus' name, amen.

Truth for the Woman in the Fire

The fire is not proof that God has left you.
It may be proof that He is refining you.
What He is forming in you is precious.

Chapter 9

The Woman Carried by Grace

There comes a point in a woman's journey when she knows she did not make it this far by her own strength.

She may have tried.
She may have fought.
She may have prayed.
She may have endured.
But when she looks back, she realizes that something greater than her own strength has been holding her all along.

That something is grace.

Grace is one of the most beautiful gifts of God.

It is His undeserved kindness.
His sustaining power.
His mercy in weakness.
His help in suffering.
His strength when ours is gone.

The woman carried by grace is not a woman who never faced pain. She is often a woman who has walked through deep valleys, long fires, and seasons she never would have chosen. She has known heartbreak, loss, waiting, weakness, and sorrow. But somehow, through all of it, she is still standing.

Not because life was easy.
Not because people were always kind.
Not because she always understood the way.

But because grace carried her.

That is what touches me so deeply about the goodness of God. He does not only save us by grace. He sustains us by grace. He keeps us by grace. He lifts us by grace. He walks with us by grace through every season we thought might break us.

Many women know what it is to be carried by grace, even if they do not always have words for it.

It is that strength that comes when you thought you had none left.
It is that peace that settles in a storm you cannot control.
It is that quiet ability to take one more step when your heart feels tired.
It is that mercy that meets you in the morning after a long night of tears.

Grace is not always loud.
Sometimes it is gentle.
Sometimes it is quiet.
Sometimes it is simply the hand of God beneath you, keeping you from falling apart.

The woman carried by grace often has a testimony she never planned to have. If she could have chosen an easier road, perhaps she would have. But now that she has come this far, she can see that grace was present in every chapter.

Grace was there in the rejection.
Grace was there in the tears.
Grace was there in the loss.
Grace was there in the weakness.
Grace was there in the fire.

Even when she did not fully see it at the time, grace was holding her.

I know something about being carried by grace.

I know and believe with all my heart that it was by the grace of God that I overcame. I have gone through pain, suffering, heartache, betrayal, and many fires, but I know I made it through those seasons because of my God. He carried me.

I remember when I was twenty-six years old, before my first husband took my children and brought them to America, I had a dream that stayed with me. In the dream, I was driving an LTD, and the road was narrow. The buildings were white, and there was a bright light in that place, but it did not hurt my eyes. I remember saying, "I want to go home." I went into a house, but it was not my home. Then I saw myself going higher and higher until it stopped.

As I looked, I saw someone carrying another person. At first, I could not see clearly. But as the person came closer, I realized the one being carried was me. I could not see His face, but I saw that He was wearing a white robe. I woke up right away and prayed, "Lord, please do not take me now, because my children are still so little."

Later, I understood that dream in a deeper way. God was showing me that there would be times in my life when I would not be able to carry myself, when I would feel too weak to walk, too broken to rise, too wounded to move forward. But in those times, He would be the One carrying me. He would walk for me when I could not walk for myself.

Not long after that, my first husband, Joel took my children and brought them to America. That pain was so deep, so sharp, and so heartbreaking that I would never wish it on anyone. But even through that agony, God helped me go on. By His grace, He carried me.

And not only through that. He carried me through being sold. He carried me through rejection. He carried me through betrayal. He carried me through bullying. Even now, when I go through hurtful things, I give them to God.

There were times when I trusted people with something tender from my heart, and instead of compassion, there was betrayal. The pain was not just in what was said. The pain was in knowing that trust had been broken. There were also people I once called close friends who turned and bullied me because of my faith. I do not drink, I do not live the way they live, and I choose to stand on the Word of God rather than on what people want. Because of that, they gave me a hard time. Even at my age, it still hurt.

But by the grace of God, I have learned that I do not have to fight every battle back. I can forgive, and I can also step away. I can love people from a distance. I can forgive without allowing continued harm. And I can trust God to be my Defender.

I forgave Joel. I forgave the people who sold me. I forgave the bullies. And even now, when people hurt me, I keep bringing that pain to the Lord. Grace has been teaching me not only how to survive, but how to forgive, how to let go, and how to keep walking with God even when my heart aches.

I know this world is full of suffering. There are still painful things we go through here on earth. But I hold on to the promise of heaven, where God will wipe away every tear. No more pain. No more sorrow. No more suffering. That promise comforts me deeply.

And because God has carried me, I can say this to other women with confidence: if He brought me through, He can bring you through too.

Grace has a way of humbling a woman in the most beautiful way. It teaches her that her survival was not her own doing alone. It teaches her that every answered prayer, every rescued moment, every new morning, every healing step, and every breath of hope was touched by the hand of God.

That realization does not make a woman weaker. It makes her more grateful.

The woman carried by grace becomes a woman who knows how to worship differently. She knows what it is to thank God not only for blessings, but for sustaining mercy. She knows how to praise Him not only for open doors, but for the strength to endure closed ones. She knows how to love Him not only because He gave her joy, but because He stayed with her in sorrow.

There is a deep beauty in that kind of faith.

Grace also softens the heart.

A woman who knows she has been carried by grace often becomes more tender toward others. She understands brokenness. She understands struggle. She understands the need for mercy. She may be stronger now, but she has not forgotten what it felt like to be weak. And because of that, she becomes a vessel of compassion.

That is one of the holy fruits of grace.

It does not only keep us alive.
It teaches us how to love.
It teaches us how to forgive.
It teaches us how to extend to others what God has so freely extended to us.

Beloved woman of God, perhaps you feel as though you barely made it here. Perhaps the road behind you is full of tears, and the road ahead still feels uncertain. Perhaps you do not feel victorious. Perhaps you only feel tired.

But if you are still here, still seeking God, still breathing, still trusting, even if only with trembling faith, then grace is already at work in your life.

You are not standing alone.
You were never standing alone.
Grace has been beneath you, around you, and ahead of you all along.

Maybe you have called it survival.
Maybe heaven calls it grace.

When God carries a woman through the fire by grace, she comes
out knowing that her life is not just a story of pain. It is a story of
mercy. It is a story of divine keeping. It is a story of a God who held
her when she could not hold herself.

And in time, she learns to say with deep humility and holy
gratitude:

I am still here because grace carried me.

Prayer

Lord,
Thank You for the grace that carries us. Thank You for every time
You held us when we were weak, strengthened us when we were
tired, and sustained us when we thought we could not go on. For
every woman reading these words, let her feel the comfort of
knowing she has not walked alone. Remind her that Your grace is
still enough for today, still enough for tomorrow, and still enough
for every fire she must walk through.
In Jesus' name, amen.

Truth for the Woman in the Fire

You are not still here by accident.
You are here because grace has carried you.
And the same grace that kept you will continue to keep you.

Chapter 10

The Woman Who Comes Out

of the Fire Stronger

Fire changes things.

It burns away what cannot remain.
It reveals what is real.
It tests what is strong.
And in the hands of God, it becomes a place where something
deeper is formed.

The woman who comes out of the fire stronger is not a woman who
escaped pain. She is a woman who walked through it. She felt the
heat. She knew the sorrow. She endured the long nights, the
unanswered questions, the tears, the losses, the betrayals, the
weakness, and the refining.

But she did not stay the same.

The fire did not destroy her.
By the grace of God, it transformed her.

There is a strength that can only be born through suffering.

It is not harsh strength.
It is not prideful strength.
It is not the strength of pretending nothing hurts.

It is holy strength.

It is the strength of a woman who has wept and still believes.
The strength of a woman who has been betrayed and still forgives.
The strength of a woman who has been wounded and still loves
God.
The strength of a woman who has walked through deep valleys
and still lifts her eyes to heaven.

That kind of strength is beautiful in the sight of God.

When a woman first enters the fire, she often feels afraid. She does
not know what will remain when the flames have done their work.
She wonders if she will survive the pain, if her faith will hold, if her
heart will ever heal, if joy will ever return.

But little by little, something begins to happen.

Her roots go deeper.
Her prayers grow stronger.
Her discernment becomes sharper.
Her dependence on God becomes more real.
Her voice becomes steadier.
Her compassion becomes deeper.
Her faith becomes less fragile and more anchored in who God is.

This is how God brings strength out of sorrow.

The woman who comes out of the fire stronger may still carry scars, but she no longer wears them with shame. She understands now that scars are not proof that God failed her. They are evidence that He brought her through.

She may still remember the pain, but the pain no longer owns her. She may still grieve what was lost, but grief no longer rules her. She may still feel the tenderness of old wounds, but those wounds are no longer in charge of her identity.

She has changed.

Not into a harder woman,
but into a deeper woman.

She has learned what matters.
She has learned where strength really comes from.
She has learned that God is faithful in the flames.

This chapter is not about a woman becoming strong so she can boast in herself. It is about a woman who knows that every step she took through the fire was made possible by God. She is stronger now, not because she became self-sufficient, but because she has learned how to lean more fully on the Lord.

That is one of the greatest miracles of spiritual strength.

It does not make a woman less dependent on God.
It makes her more dependent on Him.
It makes her know Him more deeply.
It makes her trust Him more fully.
It makes her love Him more dearly.

I know something about that kind of strength.

When I look back over my life, I know the fire was real. The pain was real. The tears were real. The rejection was real. The betrayal was real. The loss was real. The suffering was real. But I also know this: God was real in every bit of it. He did not leave me in the fire. He brought me through it.

I have been through pain that could have made me bitter.
I have been through sorrow that could have made me give up.
I have been through rejection that could have made me close my heart.
I have been through betrayal that could have made me stop trusting God.

But by His grace, I am still here.

And I am not the same woman I was before the fire.

The fire made me pray more deeply.
It made me cling to Jesus more closely.
It made me see people differently.
It made me treasure the Word of God more.
It made me understand suffering in a way I never could have understood it otherwise.
It made me more compassionate toward hurting people.
It made me more aware that every breath, every step, and every victory belongs to God.

That is what holy strength looks like.

It is not loud.
It is not proud.
It is not self-made.

It is the quiet strength of a woman who has been carried by grace, refined by fire, healed by mercy, and sustained by the presence of God.

There are women reading this who may still be in the fire right now. You may not yet feel stronger. You may feel tired, bruised, uncertain, or worn down. You may still be wondering how your story could ever look beautiful again.

Beloved woman of God, do not lose heart.

Strength is still being formed in you.
Even now.
Even here.
Even in this hard place.

God is doing something in you that cannot be seen all at once. He is building endurance. He is forming faithfulness. He is growing courage. He is deepening trust. He is shaping a testimony that will one day speak life to someone else.

The fire is not the end of your story.

You will come through.
You will not remain here forever.
And by the grace of God, you will not come out empty.

You will come out deeper.
You will come out wiser.
You will come out more discerning.
You will come out more rooted in Christ.
You will come out stronger.

Not stronger because life was gentle,
but stronger because God was faithful.

The enemy may have meant the fire to break you, but God is able to use it to build something in you that hell cannot destroy. What once made you tremble can become the place where your testimony grows. What once looked like ruin can become the ground where resilience, faith, and worship rise.

This is the strength that comes from walking with God through suffering.

It is the strength to keep loving.
The strength to keep forgiving.
The strength to keep believing.
The strength to keep standing.
The strength to keep pointing others to Jesus.

And when God carries a woman all the way through the fire, she comes out knowing with humble certainty:

I went in broken, but by the grace of God, I came out stronger.

Prayer

Lord,
For every woman who is walking through the fire, strengthen her
today. Remind her that the flames will not have the final word.
Build in her a strength that comes from Your presence, not from her
own striving. Heal what has been wounded, steady what has been
shaken, and complete the work You are doing in her. Let her come
through this fire with deeper faith, greater peace, and a stronger
heart anchored in You.
In Jesus' name, amen.

Truth for the Woman in the Fire

The fire did not mean God had left you.
It became the place where He strengthened you.
By His grace, you will come out stronger.

Conclusion

You Were Never Alone in the Fire

If there is one truth I pray every woman carries with her after reading these pages, it is this:

You were never alone in the fire.

Not in the rejection.
Not in the tears.
Not in the loss.
Not in the silence.
Not in the weakness.
Not in the refining.
Not in the long nights when your heart ached and your soul grew tired.

God was there.

He was there when no one else saw your pain.
He was there when your tears fell in private.
He was there when you felt misunderstood, overlooked, or forgotten.
He was there when your heart was breaking.
He was there when the road felt too long and the burden too heavy.

And He is still there now.

Sometimes when we walk through fire, we think the greatest miracle would be for God to keep us from it. But often, the deeper miracle is that He walks with us through it. He does not always remove the flames immediately, but He stays with us in them. He carries us, strengthens us, refines us, comforts us, and reminds us that we belong to Him.

That is what I have learned in my own life.

There were many fires I never would have chosen.
There were sorrows I never wanted to carry.
There were tears I never thought I would cry.
There were moments when I felt weak, wounded, rejected, or deeply alone.

But looking back now, I can say with all my heart that God never left me.

He was with me when I was a little girl and did not know where I would sleep.
He was with me when I was hungry.
He was with me when I was sold.
He was with me in the grief, the betrayal, the bullying, and the pain.
He was with me when my children were taken.
He was with me when my body suffered.
He was with me in the lonely places.
He was with me when I was too weak to keep going.

And He is the reason I am still here.

This book was not written to say that fire does not hurt. It does hurt. Deeply. Sometimes more than words can explain. But it was written to testify that **the fire does not have the final word. God does.**

He is the God who sees.
He is the God who hears.
He is the God who heals.
He is the God who strengthens.
He is the God who carries.
He is the God who stays.

So, if you are in the fire right now, I want to tell you what I have learned through my own journey:

Do not lose heart.
Do not believe the lie that you have been abandoned.
Do not let pain convince you that God is absent.
Do not let sorrow tell you your story is over.

The Lord is still writing.

He is still working in places you cannot yet see.
He is still holding you even when you feel weak.
He is still speaking truth over your life even when the world speaks otherwise.
He is still able to bring beauty from ashes, hope from heartbreak, and strength from suffering.

And one day, you will look back and see that what felt like the end was not the end at all. It was a place where God met you more deeply than ever before.

Maybe you entered the fire feeling broken.
Maybe you entered it feeling afraid.
Maybe you entered it feeling empty, betrayed, wounded, or forgotten.

But if you keep walking with God, you will not come out the same.

You will come out deeper.
You will come out stronger.
You will come out wiser.
You will come out more rooted in truth.
You will come out knowing your God in a way you could not have known Him without the fire.

That does not mean you will be perfect. It means you will be held. It means you will be refined. It means you will have a testimony that points beyond yourself and back to the faithfulness of God.

That is my prayer for you.

I pray that when the fire feels hot, you will remember His presence.
I pray that when the tears come, you will remember He sees them.
I pray that when weakness overwhelms you, you will remember His grace is enough.
I pray that when the enemy whispers lies, you will remember the truth of who you are in Christ.
I pray that when life hurts deeply, you will still know that God is good.
And I pray that through every season, you will hold tightly to Jesus.

Because in the end, He is the One who carried us all along.

And one day, when all the fires of this life are over, we will stand in His presence where there will be no more pain, no more sorrow, no more rejection, no more betrayal, and no more tears. What a glorious promise that is. What a faithful God we serve.

Until that day, let us keep walking.
Let us keep trusting.
Let us keep praying.
Let us keep forgiving.
Let us keep loving.
Let us keep telling the world that Jesus is still Savior, still Healer, still Deliverer, and still Lord.

You were never alone in the fire.
Not then.
Not now.
Not ever.

The same God who brought you through before will carry you through again.

Final Prayer

Lord,
Thank You for being with us in every fire. Thank You for never leaving us, never forsaking us, and never letting go of us. Thank You for Your grace, Your mercy, Your strength, and Your love. For every woman who reads this book, remind her that she is seen, held, loved, and never alone. Carry her through every trial, strengthen her in every weakness, and let her life become a testimony of Your faithfulness.
In Jesus' name, amen.

About the Author

Dr. Lende Click is a Christian author, speaker, counselor, and founder of **Lende Click Publishing**. She writes faith-filled books that encourage women, children, and families to grow in courage, healing, identity, and trust in God.

Born and raised in Cebu, Philippines, Dr. Click's life has been marked by trials, grace, healing, and redemption. Through many fires, she has seen the faithfulness of God again and again. Her testimony and ministry are rooted in the belief that the Lord brings beauty from ashes, strength from suffering, and purpose from pain.

Through her writing, Dr. Click seeks to encourage hearts, strengthen faith, and remind readers that God is present even in life's hardest seasons. She is the author of several inspirational Christian books, Bible studies, devotionals, children's books, and faith-based stories, including works from the **Faith & Courage** collection and books for women seeking spiritual growth, healing, and restoration.

In addition to writing, Dr. Click serves as a Christian counselor. She is an **NCCA Licensed Professional Clinical Counselor, Certified Temperament Counselor, NCCA Licensed Clinical Pastoral Counselor,** and **NCCA Licensed Christian Counselor**. She is also advanced certified in **Death and Grief Therapy** and **Integrated Marriage and Family Therapy,** and she is a member of the **American Association of Christian Counselors (AACC)** and the **National Christian Counselors Association (NCCA)**.

Dr. Click writes with a special heart for women who are hurting, children in need, and those who long to know God more deeply. Through her books and ministry, she desires to point every reader to Jesus Christ — the One who saves, restores, carries, and never leaves His children alone in the fire.

Some proceeds from her work help support children in Cebu, Philippines. She currently lives in Augusta, Georgia, and continues to write books that inspire faith, courage, healing, and hope.

Ministry / Mission

This book was born out of prayer, pain, healing, and the faithfulness of God.

It was written to encourage women, lift up the hurting, and point every heart back to **Jesus Christ**—the One who never leaves us alone in the fire.

But this book also carries another burden close to my heart: the precious children of **Cebu, Philippines**.

I know what it is to be hungry.
I know what it is to feel forgotten.
I know what it is to need help and hope.

That is why some proceeds from this book go toward helping children in **Cebu, Philippines**, as the Lord provides. My desire is to share not only words of faith but also acts of love—so that children in need may feel the kindness, care, and compassion of God through His people.

Thank you for helping make that possible through your prayers and support.

My prayer is that this book will not only bless your life but will also become part of God's blessing in the life of someone else.

Other Books by Dr. Lende Click

The Gift of Godly Friendship
A Bible study for women who long for meaningful, godly connection.

Daughters of the King
An 8-week Bible study workbook for women growing in faith, identity, and purpose.

Prayers of a Daughter of the King
A devotional journey of prayer, strength, and deeper intimacy with God.

God Is Still Writing Your Story
A faith-filled message of hope for those learning to trust God in unfinished seasons.

When God Carries a Woman Through the Fire
A powerful encouragement for women walking through pain, testing, and restoration.

A Life Redeemed
A story of God's grace, healing, and redeeming love.

Serving the Lord with a Willing Heart
A 12-Week Bible Study on Faithful Service for the Lord

Healing for the Woman Who Has Been Hurt
A Bible Study for Finding Hope, Restoration, and Wholeness in Christ

Faith & Courage Children's Books

Sammy the Shy Snail's Big Race
A gentle story of courage, faith, and believing God can help you do hard things.

Bella the Brave Butterfly and the Stormy Day
A sweet story teaching children courage and trust in God during fearful times.

Toby the Turtle Who Trusted God
A faith-filled story about learning to trust God one step at a time.

Lende's Story: Faith Like Sunshine
An uplifting story of faith, hope, and God's light shining through every season.

Christian Fantasy

The Kingdom of Everlight
An epic faith-filled fantasy story of courage, destiny, and the triumph of light over darkness.

Book One in The Kingdom of Everlight Series

The Kingdom of Everlight: The Crown of Hidden Fire

An Epic Christian Fantasy of Courage, Sacrifice, and the Light That Darkness Cannot Destroy

Book Two in The Kingdom of Everlight Series